Big Data and Machine Learning

by Brett S. Martin

Cover: Facilities with large numbers of powerful computers make big data and machine learning possible.

Norwood House Press
P.O. Box 316598
Chicago, Illinois 60631

For information regarding Norwood House Press, please visit our website at.
www.norwoodhousepress.com or call 866-565-2900.

PHOTO CREDITS: Cover: © Scanrail1/Shutterstock Images; © Akhenaton Images/Shutterstock Images, 29; © Alexander Kirch/Shutterstock Images, 33; © Andrew Matthews/Press Association/PA Wire URN:30099549/AP Images, 12; © Bunditinay/Shutterstock Images, 28; © Chris Radburn/Press Association/PA Wire URN:28954785/AP Images, 37; © dotstock/Shutterstock Images, 16; © Eric Risberg/AP Images, 36; © Everett Collection/Shutterstock Images, 9; © Gorodenkoff/Shutterstock Images, 25; © Henny Ray Abrams/AP Images, 42; © Jon Simon/Feature Photo Service for IBM/AP Images, 38; © Kaspars Grinvalds/Shutterstock Images, 14; © Kite_rin/Shutterstock Images, 10; © Mark Agnor/Shutterstock Images, 23; © mavo/Shutterstock Images, 5; © Michael Dwyer/AP Images, 32; © Pe3k/Shutterstock Images, 19; © Pierre-Olivier/Shutterstock Images, 40; © rawpixel.com/Shutterstock Images, 21; © Wdnet Creation/Shutterstock Images, 18; © Worawee Meepian/Shutterstock Images, 26

Content Consultant: Jake Williams, Assistant Professor, Information Science, Drexel University

Hardcover ISBN: 978-1-59953-938-6
Paperback ISBN: 978-1-68404-217-3

© 2019 by Norwood House Press.

Library of Congress Cataloging-in-Publication Data

Names: Martin, Brett S., author.
Title: Big data and machine learning / by Brett Martin.
Description: Chicago, Illinois : Norwood House Press, [2018] | Series: Tech bytes |
   Includes bibliographical references and index.
Identifiers: LCCN 2018003241 (print) | LCCN 2018011594 (ebook) | ISBN
   9781684042227 (ebook) | ISBN 9781599539386 (hardcover : alk. paper) | ISBN
   9781684042173 (pbk. : alk. paper)
Subjects: LCSH: Big data--Juvenile literature. | Machine learning--Juvenile literature.
Classification: LCC QA76.9.B45 (ebook) | LCC QA76.9.B45 M37 2018 (print) |
   DDC 005.7--dc23
LC record available at https://lccn.loc.gov/2018003241

312N—072018
Manufactured in the United States of America in North Mankato, Minnesota.

CONTENTS

Note: Words that are **bolded** in the text are defined in the glossary.

CHAPTER 1

An Explosion of Big Data

A young woman is walking downtown. As she passes her favorite department store, her smartphone beeps. The store's computer system knows she is close by. It tracks her shopping habits. The computer system is aware that she recently bought a new coat. It knows that many people who buy a coat also buy a scarf. So, the store sends a coupon for a scarf to her phone. But she is not interested in shopping. Instead, she walks down a block to the coffee shop.

Her phone beeps again. The coffee shop's mobile app knows she is in the store. She pulls her coffee shop loyalty card up on the app. She has earned a free drink. Otherwise, she would have paid with the app.

Drink in hand, she gets comfortable in a chair. She sets up her laptop. Then she logs on to a social media website. She sends messages to her friends. The site shows her people it thinks she might know. It asks if she wants to connect

Personalized coupons are just one way stores use shoppers' data.

with them. Some are coworkers. Others are friends of friends. While sipping her coffee, she browses the site. She makes a new connection then likes a local bakery's page. Almost immediately, a coupon pops up. If she buys a cake from the bakery today, she'll get 15 percent off.

From the department store to the social media network, the woman's entire experience is closely linked with big data and machine learning. Big data is a body of information that is large and varied. Big data is generated very quickly. It can be challenging to **analyze** and interpret. But with the right tools, big data can be extremely valuable. Machine learning is when computer systems are trained to learn on their own. Humans program the computers to learn. But they do not tell

Location-Based Advertising

Advertising was very different before the Internet. Companies often placed expensive ads in newspapers. The entire newspaper readership would see the same ad. Today, a personalized online ad can be sent to an audience of one. This is partially because of big data. It allows companies to advertise by specific location. Data from a person's phone tells his or her location. The data alerts companies when the customer is close to the store. The company's computer system automatically sends an ad to the customer. The goal is to draw the person inside to spend money.

them what to do. They learn by looking at data.

When big data and machine learning work together, the result can seem like magic. **Geolocation** data from the woman's phone told the store she was nearby. When she went online, the social network identified people she might know. This was based on her profile.

The site looked at where she went to college and worked. It looked at who she sent messages to. It used this data to recommend new connections.

A Short History of Big Data

People have kept and analyzed records, or data, since prehistoric times. Ancient humans made notches in sticks and bones. They did this to keep track of food and other supplies. Around 2400 BCE, the abacus was invented. The abacus is a device with beads that slide along strings or rods. It helps people do math. The origin is still in dispute. Some historians say it was invented in China. Others credit the Babylonians or Egyptians. Ancient Greeks invented another early calculating device between 100 and 200 CE. Called the Antikythera mechanism, it had gears to track the solar system.

In 1663, statistician John Graunt used data to warn where the bubonic plague would strike. He noticed trends in where people were dying. He identified the locations and people most at risk of infection.

In the 1880s, a young engineer at the US Census Bureau invented a machine. Herman Hollerith's device was called a tabulating machine. The machine punched holes in paper cards, then counted the results. The technology analyzed census data in three months. The project would have taken ten years without the device. Hollerith went on to start the technology company IBM.

In the 1960s, government researchers wanted to share information more easily. In 1962, researcher Joseph Carl Robnett Licklider at the Massachusetts Institute of Technology (MIT) made a proposal. He wanted to connect computers together to share data.

Meanwhile, companies started developing technologies that became

The Rise of the Internet

It is hard to imagine life today without the Internet. Many people use it daily. But it did not start out as a way for people to access information. In the 1960s, computers were large and immovable. Sharing data between computers required sending computer tapes through the mail. In 1965, a computer scientist at MIT connected two computers. One was in Massachusetts, and the other was in California. They connected over a phone line. This network was called Advanced Research Projects Agency Network, or ARPANET. This network became the Internet.

supercomputers. Supercomputers are fast, high-performance systems. They can process data very quickly. Work that would take a human thousands of years to complete takes a supercomputer only a few seconds. The Advanced Scientific Computer was one of the first supercomputers. Texas Instruments designed it between 1966 and 1973.

By 1965, connecting computers had made it possible to collect large amounts of data. That year, the US government proposed the first large **data center**. It wanted the data center to store 742 million tax returns. It was also supposed to store 175 million sets of fingerprints. The government planned to store the data on **magnetic computer tape**. These tapes would be stored in one location. However, the government dropped the project. The public worried about a potential invasion of people's privacy.

In 1989, the term *big data* first appeared in *Harper's Magazine*. This data was mostly customer data, such as people's addresses. Companies would use the data to send people marketing materials.

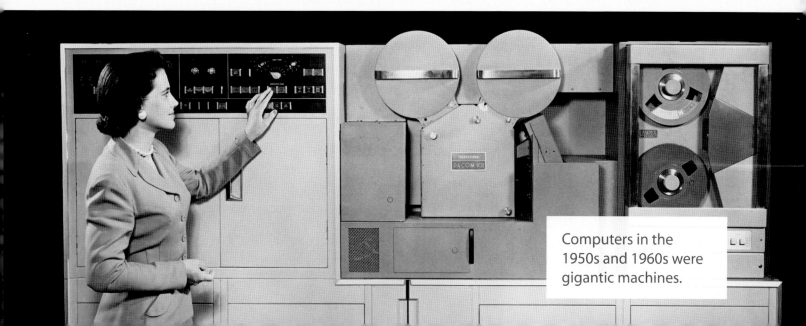

Computers in the 1950s and 1960s were gigantic machines.

Every time you use the Internet, you leave behind a trail of data.

This became known as junk mail. This was not big data as it is known today.

The World Wide Web is the most commonly used part of the Internet. The web became public in 1991. It connected people around the globe. This changed how people shopped and communicated. Internet users still create a lot of data.

We Produce and Consume Big Data Every Day

People across the planet produce data every single second. Everyday activities create data. Using a mobile phone or social media site creates data. Booking a hotel or airline flight online produces data. Every time people log on to the Internet, they produce new data. So much information coming from so many sources has led to big data.

Data is coming from more places than ever before. Data sources are constantly growing. Trillions of devices called **sensors** now produce data. Vehicles, utility grids, and almost any new piece of machinery can have sensors. Big data is all of this information combined together.

Businesses use big data for many purposes. It makes marketing more effective. Companies can track patterns in what customers buy. This helps them design products or add features they know people want. Media companies use data to know what TV shows people like.

This lets them create new shows their audiences will enjoy.

Individual people also use big data. It can be used to recommend movies based on the movies a person has liked in the past. Banking applications allow people to see years of their own financial data. They can see how much they made and how much they spent in the last month,

DID YOU KNOW?

The amount companies spent on location-based advertising jumped from $1.6 billion in 2013 to nearly $15 billion in 2018.

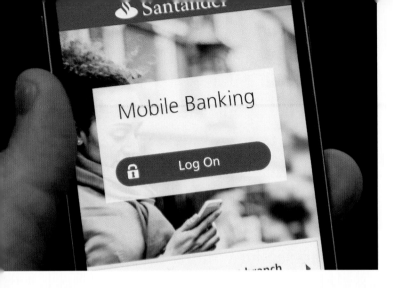

Many people use the Internet and big data to track their money.

year, or decade. They can use the data to make a budget for the future. Big data also lets people monitor their own health. The ways people use big data are always expanding.

Unlocking the Value of Big Data

For data to be useful, it must be analyzed. Programmers create computer software that finds useful patterns or connections. This process is known as analytics.

Machine learning is a common type of analytics. As machines see new data, they learn more. Faster computers can learn more quickly. Machine learning can apply complex math formulas to big data. It can find new information by analyzing big data. Machine learning can find patterns in data that human analysts fail to see.

Companies can use the information to understand what customers will buy. A common use of machine learning is online recommendations. When people shop online, the online store will show related products based on their searches. This data is from other shoppers who performed similar searches. This is machine learning at work with big data.

Machine learning has helped people communicate with one another. Language translation programs use machine learning to improve their translations. Translation programs train on data from thousands of translated texts. The data includes text in dozens of languages. Then the programs analyze patterns in the data. They use the patterns to decide how to translate a sentence from one language to another.

Data at Your Fingertips

With so much data available, everyone can do tasks that used to require specialists. Travel agents used to book flights, hotels, or vacations for families. Apps now help people find the best deals. Personal devices tell people about their diet, sleep, and exercise. People can compare their results with others. They can also see whether they are meeting their goals.

Consumers have shopped online for more than 20 years. Now, apps use big data to let people track prices, find coupons, and comparison shop. Other apps notify people when favorite items are on sale. As big data grows, so do the ways people can use it.

Big data helps runners track their health and progress.

CHAPTER 2

Solving Big Data Challenges

Big data has presented opportunities and challenges. Analyzing data helps researchers and companies gain valuable insights. But it is difficult to store so much information. Another challenge is analyzing it and getting results quickly. Big data also raises privacy and security issues.

Organizing Big Data

Any action a person or company does online produces data. Even something as basic as entering search words in Google can provide useful data. Companies collect all this data. But it is not organized so they can use it.

Unstructured data poses its own challenges. It includes pictures, audio, and videos. Unlike a number, a piece of unstructured data has no clear meaning to a computer. People can easily spot a shape. But computers must be taught how to do this. This makes the data hard to search and analyze.

Companies store the data they collect in large computers called servers.

To solve this problem, companies use analytics tools. Data scientists tell the analytics tools what to look for. These computer programs look through all the data. Then the programs organize the data. They look for patterns that may be useful for companies.

Analyzing Big Data

Even with analytics tools, analyzing big data is a challenge. Researchers struggle to develop tools powerful enough to look at data in such large volumes.

One solution is data visualization. Special software programs perform data visualization. They turn raw data into pictures, graphs, or charts. A basic pie chart can show the percentage of people who opened an e-mail. A more complex chart can show national sales data. Companies can compare sales figures across the country. Companies can use the chart to see where consumers want to buy their product.

Showing data visually, rather than as text, lets viewers quickly notice patterns and trends. Anyone can look at the visual and understand the data right away. Some types of visualizations are interactive. Users may be able to zoom in on a map for a more detailed view. They may be able to touch one part of a chart to get more information.

Insights from analytics help companies make decisions. The AMC channel makes hit TV shows. The company uses complex data analytics tools to understand its customers. It uses these tools to decide what shows to advertise throughout the week. It does not just collect data from

Finding Flu

Millions of people search Google for flu symptoms. This gave the technology company an idea. In 2008, it started collecting data from all flu symptom searches. This data included the locations of the people searching for flu symptoms. Then it created an **algorithm** that estimated where the flu was spreading. At first, its estimates were very accurate. This helped health-care organizations treat and contain the flu. But over the next few years, the algorithm was not as effective at analyzing new data. The results were not as helpful. Google ended its flu trend program in 2014.

its cable TV channel. It collects data from its online channel, its app, and third-party streaming programs.

Most organizations use big data and analytics. Even video game companies use them. Game designers use machine-learning algorithms. Game companies record every single player

Big data can uncover trends, from flu outbreaks to buying habits.

> ### **?** **DID YOU KNOW?**
>
> **Approximately 2.6 exabytes (2.6 billion gigabytes) of data are produced worldwide every day. This is enough to store 530 million songs.**

action in a game. They analyze the data to improve the games. Blizzard makes the popular online game *World of Warcraft*. In the game, players can battle each other. The game collects data on how well players do. Then it uses an algorithm to pair up players fairly. Data can also tell game companies which players are most likely to spend money to play or pay for upgrades.

Keeping Personal Data Private

Some people do not want organizations to look at their data. They do not want others to know what websites they visited.

Young men play the popular game *World of Warcraft* at a gaming convention.

Protecting Personal Data

Personal data is information that could identify a living person. It could be someone's name or home address. Banking information is also considered personal data. So is medical information. In the United States, there is no single federal law that protects personal data. Instead, this protection is covered by a mix of federal and state laws. Sometimes these laws agree on what data to protect and how. But other times, they disagree. It can be tricky for consumers and law enforcement to know when laws have been broken.

They want to keep their social media contacts and other personal details private.

One way companies keep personal data private is anonymization. A wireless provider may collect a person's mobile phone number, full name, home address, and credit card information. Data anonymization would remove the person's name and street address. This would make it harder to trace the phone number back to the individual. But anonymization alone does not fully protect personal data. Companies collect a lot of personal data. Just three or four pieces of information can make the data identifiable. Companies must also store personal information securely. They may use **firewalls** or password-protected databases.

Data privacy laws protect people's data. Companies must tell consumers what data they collect. They also have to share how they use consumers' data. Consumers must agree to let companies collect or use their data before using a product or service. However, only 16 percent of people read companies' privacy policies. They may be giving away their rights to privacy without knowing it. This is a growing problem.

Few people read company privacy policies that explain how companies protect and use data.

Bringing Dark Data into the Light

With so much data available, organizations cannot use it all. The unused information is called dark data. Any data that an organization has but does not use can be called dark data. It can include old or deleted files. Researchers and companies might store this data. But they do not always analyze or process it. Cost is one reason. Analytics tools are expensive. Organizations do not want to invest in them unless they know the data has value.

But a new technology is helping organizations store and use the

DID YOU KNOW?

Up to 90 percent of a company's big data is dark data.

information. Data lakes are storage centers that can store all types of data in their original formats. Data lakes help store data cheaply. They can hold the data until a company is ready to use it. Sometimes the data is stored unused for several years.

Securing Big Data

Another challenge with big data is how to secure it. Some is stored at a company's data centers. Other data is stored online in the **cloud**. This data is not stored in a single location. Instead, it is distributed across networks to locations across the United States and the world. This makes it very challenging to secure.

Companies can do several things to meet this challenge. First, they can encrypt their data. Encryption is like a secret code. It takes readable data and scrambles it up. Only computers with the encryption key can make sense of the data. Encryption protects data as it moves from system to system. Companies can also set up security measures around the data. Requiring passwords to log in to data storage systems can prevent information from being stolen. So can installing and updating security software.

Companies also create disaster recovery plans for their data. These plans outline how companies will recover and protect data if someone steals it or it is lost. At data centers, physical security is used. Sturdy walls and locked entry points keep people out. The largest data centers even have armed guards protecting them.

Data centers are large facilities that house servers full of data.

CHAPTER 3

Putting Big Data and Machine Learning to Work

Big data and machine learning have become part of everyday life. This data does not just tell companies and people what happened in the past. It helps banks fight **fraud** and social media companies stop bullying. **Wearable technology** puts big data at people's fingertips. Today, big data and machine learning are even helping to predict what will happen in the future.

Fighting Fraud with Big Data

Fraud costs companies and customers billions of dollars each year. And it is becoming more sophisticated. It is more difficult for humans to discover and prevent.

Machine learning and big data offer a solution. Just like all humans, criminals are creatures of habit. They tend to use the

Bank security professionals use machine learning to identify fraud.

same combination of tactics to steal data. Or they may steal certain information during a specific time of year. Tax data is more likely to be stolen during tax season, for example. Banks and other financial companies use big data and machine learning to find and keep track of these patterns.

Fraud prevention can find and flag instances that appear to be fraudulent. It can also find and flag when new accounts are opened or applied for. Fraud prevention teams can identify cases that

Social media platforms such as Twitter can produce valuable data.

have links to crime. Uncovering these connections in data shows when a request for money could be related to fraud.

To be effective, fraud detection software must be fast. Machine learning can help keep the process fast. Software learns and adapts on its own. Using data, banks can find and fix fraud much faster than any human ever could.

Social Media

Social media creates a lot of big data. Every day, Twitter users produce more than 500 million tweets. Facebook users produce more than 4.5 billion likes each day. Each tweet and like produces useful data. Companies find trends in the data about what their customers like or do not like. They use it to improve their product or service.

But big data from social media can serve another important purpose. It can identify social issues such as cyberbullying. Data analysis can identify bullying text on social media sites such as Twitter and YouTube. Researchers map the data to see where bullying occurs. Finding where the problem happens is the first step toward stopping it. The same approach also helps find terrorist activities. The data identify people who are in known terrorist networks. Then law enforcement can monitor their activities.

A Wave of Wearable Technology

Wearable technology devices are gadgets people wear. Some are worn on the wrist

Data Scientists

The term *data scientist* was coined in 2008. The job has been in demand ever since. Data scientists make sense of big data. They use math, statistics, and programming to organize data. Then they analyze it to answer tough questions. The career website Glassdoor ranked data scientist as the best job in the United States in 2016. Data scientists tend to make high salaries. Plus, there are many job openings.

The Apple Watch can tell wearers if their heart rhythm becomes irregular.

like watches. Others look like necklaces. Some wearable technology is built right into clothing. These devices connect to the Internet or a smartphone. They produce lots of data about the person wearing them. Fitness trackers record how many steps someone takes each day. They may monitor the wearer's heart rate, sleep patterns, and calories burned. Apps connected to the trackers give wearers suggestions about how to improve. The data helps people build and maintain healthy habits.

Wearable devices produce a lot of data. Companies and researchers are just starting to understand how to use it. Doctors are using data from fitness trackers to help patients catch health conditions before they become serious. And wearable tech companies use the data to improve their devices. The Apple Heart Study app connects to the Apple Watch. The watch detects the wearer's heart rhythms. It sends this data to the app. If the app detects an irregular pattern, it sends this data back to the watch. The watch buzzes on the wearer's wrist. It warns the wearer that an irregular heart rhythm is happening. The wearer can then schedule a doctor's appointment or visit the hospital.

Apps are fun, but people should be aware of the way in which some apps track their users.

Smartphones and Big Data

Smartphones let people access information anywhere and anytime. When users visit websites on their smartphones, data is created. The websites collect where

DID YOU KNOW? ?

Companies sold 80 million wearable tech devices in 2015.

DID YOU KNOW?

App stores offer hundreds of thousands of apps. They use big data to find the apps individual users might want to download.

they are and the web pages they visit. Smartphone apps run constantly. These apps also produce data. They track users' locations, social media habits, and even movements.

Analyzing smartphone data gives insights into people's behavior. This information helps websites and apps deliver a better product. It also helps them sell more products and services. However, users may not like their personal data being used in this way.

Knowing What Will Happen before It Happens

In the past, data analytics could only show what had already happened. Sales data shows the top products stores have sold. This helps companies know how much of a product to ship to each store. But predictive analytics allow organizations to guess what will happen in the future. Predictive analytics use algorithms and machine learning. Outcomes can be predicted based on new and historical

Data Security

Data breaches happen when data is lost or stolen. The data can include peoples' Social Security numbers, driver's license numbers, medical records, or banking information. Criminals can use this information to steal someone's identity. More than 9 billion data records have been lost or stolen since 2013. Major data breaches can cost companies millions of dollars.

data. Researchers and analysts use the data to forecast future behavior and trends.

A European train company uses predictive analytics. It analyzes data to know when train parts will fail. It uses data from trains, repair and maintenance schedules, the weather, and the supply chain. Replacing parts before they fail keeps trains running on time. On some routes, only 1 percent of trains are ever delayed.

Automatic Fixes

Prescriptive analytics go beyond making predictions. They make recommendations to solve problems. The analytics combine machine learning, artificial intelligence, and other technologies.

The retailer Target was the victim of a massive data breach in 2014.

Few organizations use prescriptive analytics. But those that do gain a lot of benefits. Prescriptive analytics make recommendations on scheduling and ordering products. This helps get the right products to the right places at the right time.

The analytics can offer **probabilities**. These tell companies the chance something will happen. For instance, banks use prescriptive analytics for some loans. The analytics look at all available data to determine if a person is likely or unlikely to repay the loan.

CHAPTER 4

A Future of Possibilities

The use of big data is growing rapidly. Organizations will use big data and machine learning to uncover new opportunities. Soon, most companies will use big data if they do not already. The number of smart devices in the Internet of Things will continue to grow and produce data. Automobile companies will use big data and machine learning to perfect self-driving cars. Big data will help doctors improve health

The Internet of Things includes smart appliances that can be controlled from devices such as tablets.

care. And artificial intelligence will uncover even more opportunities.

Billions of Connected Devices

One reason for the explosion of data is the Internet of Things (IoT). The IoT is made up of all the devices around the world that connect to the Internet. This includes household items such as refrigerators and thermostats. But it also includes smart streetlights and parking meters. Farmers use the IoT to monitor crops. Factories use the IoT to improve efficiency. All of these devices produce and share data without humans being involved.

Approximately 80 billion devices will be connected in 2025. Those devices will produce approximately 10 percent of the world's data. Organizations will need new,

Moving to the Cloud

The cloud has become a popular place to store data. People can access data on the cloud from any device with an Internet connection. Companies and people like the cloud because it is cheaper than storing data on their own computers. With more data being stored, it is no surprise that cloud usage is on the rise. In 2020, 92 percent of data will be stored in the cloud.

faster ways to collect, analyze, and use big data from the IoT. Machine learning will be a big part of this innovation. Smart devices will be designed to learn on their own using data from millions of connected devices.

Self-Driving Cars

Big data and machine learning help make self-driving cars possible. These cars are covered in a wide variety of sensors. Sensors monitor the car's speed, its direction, and whether it is braking. A GPS tells the car its location. Sensors recognize traffic signals and objects on the road, including cars, bikes, and people. Together, these sensors generate vast amounts of data at all times. Computers

inside the car must process that data as fast as possible to ensure a safe ride.

Car manufacturers employ machine learning to improve the performance of self-driving cars. They use data collected from thousands of vehicles to design safety updates. These updates improve crash avoidance and safety without requiring a driver to take action.

People check out the Waymo driverless car at a 2016 Google event.

Self-driving cars may reduce accidents caused by human error. They could also reduce traffic and free up the time people spend commuting. Consumers will soon be able to purchase self-driving cars. Some analysts predict babies born in 2017 will never need to learn how to drive. Self-driving cars will be the norm.

Personalized Health Care

Big data is helping doctors improve health care. People have different **genetic** makeups. Big data helps doctors understand their patients' genetics. They can quickly identify patients who would be good candidates for a particular drug.

A person's health history, lifestyle, and location provide useful data. The data can tell doctors if a person is at risk of a disease. Doctors can even provide treatment before a patient has symptoms.

Machine learning can predict when patients have a disease. When people are not feeling well, they often enter their symptoms into a search engine. This lets them see possible causes and treatments. Machine learning can identify patients who may have serious conditions, such as cancer, before they are even diagnosed. Machine learning is also helping hospitals improve their operations. Software analyzes how long patients stay in the hospital. It uses this data to free up hospital beds and improve care.

Scientist Stephen Hawking presented at a conference on artificial intelligence in 2016.

Doctors in Japan used this type of machine learning to find rare cancers. In 2016, a group of doctors in Tokyo had a difficult case. Their treatment had not worked for their patient. They did not know what type of cancer their patient had.

The doctors turned to big data and machine learning. They used IBM's

Data scientist Eric Clark shows off wearable tech that could monitor the health of people with Parkinson's disease.

to diagnose their patient. Their new treatment was successful.

Deep Learning and Artificial Intelligence

Deep learning is a type of machine learning. Deep learning makes sense of unstructured data such as images, sound, and text. It recognizes voice commands. This is what robots use when they respond to people telling them what to do.

Artificial intelligence (AI) is part of computer science. Its goal is to have

supercomputer Watson. Watson is very fast and powerful. They told Watson their patient's symptoms. Watson then went to work. The computer scanned through 20 million cancer studies. It was looking for patterns. It found cases in the studies that had the same symptoms the doctors' patient did. The doctors used the information from Watson's analysis computers solve problems like humans do. Machine learning is one aspect of AI. Both use hardware, software, and big data. Today, companies use AI to automate processes. This means machines perform tasks on their own. Humans do not need to tell them what to do. Work gets done quickly and efficiently. Companies use AI to automatically send customers e-mails with special offers based on their Internet searches.

Eventually, researchers hope AI machines will think like humans do. This would let machines make decisions quickly without human input. They will work independently. Advanced machine learning is always evolving. New tools will make performing complex tasks easier.

Making Cities Smarter

A smart city uses data, analytics, and technology to provide better services. At the heart of a smart city are sensors. They use the IoT to share data. The data manages streetlights, traffic signals, and other electronics. This lowers energy

? DID YOU KNOW?

Soon, 85 percent of customer service interactions will be with robots, according to tech research firm Gartner. The robots will answer questions using AI.

Parking sensors within parking spaces help drivers locate open spots.

costs. During rush hour or emergencies, traffic signals can have longer or shorter red lights to avoid traffic jams. Sensors throughout the city can provide early warnings about disasters. They can alert officials to a flood, drought, landslide, or hurricane.

A smart city provides information that helps people. Smart parking meters connect to an app. The app tells drivers when parking spots are open. This helps people find parking spots right away. Drivers can also pay for their parking spots online. In the future, cars may have sensors that connect to parking meters. The sensor would tell a nearby meter where the car is. The meter would send data back to direct the car to any empty space.

In the future, sensors in the road may monitor pollution. The sensors would send this information to city officials. Officials could use the data to change traffic patterns. They could send drivers to different routes to reduce the concentration of pollution. Big data is already making cities smarter. But even more opportunities are on the horizon.

Big Data in the Classroom

Many experts expect big data and machine learning to shape the future of education. Students learn at different rates. Digital learning uses data and machine learning to personalize learning. The data can tell a teacher if a student or class is struggling to learn. Maybe students do not understand certain words in a book. Or maybe they do not understand fractions in math. The teacher can see who needs help. This helps prevent students from falling behind.

Big Data on Wall Street

Machine learning will change the stock market, too. The stock market is a place where shares of companies are bought and sold. The stock market trades billions of dollars daily. Many major financial firms use machines to perform these trades. Machines can perform more trades than humans can. The machines look at financial data and other information, such as online news. The systems use the data to make decisions on what to buy or sell. These systems are much faster than

DID YOU KNOW?

In 2017, computers made nearly 75 percent of stock market trades without human input.

Computers now perform large numbers of stock trades.

The Dangers of Machine Learning

Some people worry machine learning and AI can learn too much. If that happens, they may no longer need humans to program them. Computers could make their own decisions. That could lead to computers or robots taking over the planet. Stephen Hawking, a British scientist and author, had this concern. "Computers double their performance every 18 months. So the danger is real that they could develop intelligence and take over the world," Hawking said in an interview.

human traders or financial researchers. Experts predict humans will have little or no role in the day-to-day operation of the stock market.

Big data and machine learning are more than trends. Big data and machine learning could reveal answers to many problems. They are essential parts of daily life. Organizations will continue to use new devices and technologies that create big data. Analyzing that data will allow new innovations and discoveries for the future.

algorithm (AL-go-rith-um): A set of rules computers use to solve a problem.

analyze (AN-uh-lyz): To examine data to gain an understanding, explanation, and interpretation.

cloud (KLOWD): Data processing and storage space on the Internet.

data center (DAY-tuh sen-tur): A physical or virtual space for storing computer, server, and networking systems and data.

firewalls (FY-ur-walz): Hardware and software systems that protect computer networks from hackers.

fraud (FRAHD): Lying or making untrue claims to make money or personal gain.

genetic (gen-NET-ik): Relating to the proteins that determine an individual's physical characteristics.

geolocation (gee-oh-loh-KAY-shun): Identifying the real-world location of an object, such as a smartphone.

magnetic computer tape (mag-NED-ik kum-PEW-tur TAYP): A system for storing digital data on cartridges or cassettes.

probabilities (prah-buh-BIL-ih-tees): The chances that something will occur.

sensors (SEN-surz): Devices that detect heat, light, sound, pressure, or other changes in their environments.

wearable technology (WAYR-uh-bul tek-NOL-uh-gee): A computer or advanced electronic device worn as an accessory or item of clothing on the body.

Books

Carla Mooney. *Big Data: Information in the Digital World with Science Activities for Kids*. White River Junction, VT: Nomad Press, 2018. Learn more about how information is stored in our world and try hands-on activities related to big data.

Gloria Winquist. *Coding iPhone Apps for Kids: A Playful Introduction to Swift*. San Francisco, CA: No Starch Press, 2017. Write your own iPhone app with easy-to-follow instructions and activities.

Max Wainewright. *Code Your Own Games! 20 Games to Create with Scratch*. New York: Sterling Publishing, 2017. Try your hand at creating your own computer games.

Websites

Beanz: The Magazine for Kids, Code, and Computer Science (https://www.kidscodecs.com/) This website has hundreds of articles and resources on computers, coding, and the IoT.

Explain That Stuff (http://www.explainthatstuff.com) This website contains articles that explain complex topics such as big data, making them easy to understand.

HowStuffWorks (http://electronics.howstuffworks.com) This website provides easy-to-understand answers and explanations of how technology works. It offers great articles explaining how big data works.

INDEX

M
Massachusetts Institute of
Technology (MIT), 7, 8

P
Personal data, 19–20
Privacy policies, 21

S
Self-driving cars, 35–36
Sensors, 11, 35, 39, 40
Smart cities, 39–40
Social media, 4, 5, 10, 20, 24,
26–27, 30
Stock market, 41, 43
Supercomputers, 8, 38

T
Texas Instruments, 8
Twitter, 26, 27

U
Unstructured data, 15, 38
US Census Bureau, 7

W
Watson, 38
Wearable technology, 24, 27–29
World of Warcraft, 19
World Wide Web, 10

Y
YouTube, 27

Brett S. Martin has more than 20 years of writing experience. He has worked as a reporter, editor, director of public relations, and president of his own media company. He has written for more than two dozen magazines and has written several fiction and nonfiction books. He has also volunteered as a youth football coach for nine seasons. Martin lives in Shakopee, Minnesota, with his wife and two teenage sons.